LIFE

VICTORIA SIMON

DEDICATED TO MY LOVING SISTER CISSY

A selfless loving soul

We remember you each day

Unseen, unheard

We still miss you even today

Never will we forget you, your absence still is felt

You are loved beyond words

Without you life is not the same

Remembering you is easy

We do it everyday

Missing you is a heartache

That will never fade away.

Contents

I

Love The Life You Live

*"I asked God to give me everything I could enjoy in life.
God gave me LIFE so that I could enjoy everything."*

THE BEGINNING

The beginning is the most important part of any work. We will never be able to know unless we

begin. Life is a nourishment given to all by the Almighty. To know life is to thread your way into it

by acquainting yourself with it.

As I am expanding and writing to know life more deeply, I find there is something unique in it

which we all miss – out on, though each one of us uses it emotionally and freely to transform

our lives.

Focusing on the change of ideas on life which, keeps persistent and consistent, but which at

times seems to be a turning point that leaves an unhappy silence.
So how do we describe life?

Are we living large with life, or is it covered with a shadow of gray?

An intense thought shows we were and are living with heartbreaks, family loss, financial

hardships, illness, bereavement, depression, dejection, and of dreams unfulfilled. Is this the real

image? We all know very well that every coin has two sides and life does too. Do we ever think

of what life has given us? No..... most of it is not accommodated in our space.

What about the joy, the health, the home, the family, the presence of our parents, the promise of

God, His blessing and the beautiful world we live in. We may have missed out on a few things

unknowingly. Life is an unknown trip of ups and downs for every living being.

There is sorrow and there's joy, there's rain but sunshine too, there's darkness but brightness is

always at the horizon. Everything is connected to our state of mind, easy to break and difficult to

make. All one needs in this life is to conquer ourselves.

What we miss in life is not always important as what we find in the search of 'WHY', that's how

the saying goes (seems odd). Voicing uncherished moments will take you nowhere. Truly finding a new path will lead you somewhere. So, the best thing is to search for the light which lies at the

bend, gone unnoticed.

The rhythm of the proverb expresses that 'Every cloud has a silver lining'.

Many react without hesitation questioning, "Where is the silver lining?"

If you have the faith and courage to pursue your goal, all your dreams can come true. If you

If you miss trying, you will lose your goal.

Let us always remember that life is full of unexpected things as, it is completely a series of moments. To be living one needs to cross the hurdles, creating a happy frame of mind and

learning to live in both the bright light and the darkness. The only difference is to wake up and

open the doors of light.

Life is also an ever growing and creating workforce through many challenging requirements. A

desire for excellence, a quest to achieve higher heights without the realization that they may or

may not bring success. Sometimes it's a bright day, sometimes a dark and cloudy day.

Each expectation may not materialize moving you into a shell of depression. This upward force

of defeat and failure and doubt results in the caving in of the long-cherished ambitions.

The way to straighten life is to emerge and make an effort, every moment a new approach by

rekindling the inner light of courage to start anew. It may be difficult, not impossible.

Just remember that yesterday is not ours to recover but tomorrow we may have a treasured

chance or may get a small space in a closet, but we need to keep in mind that today is the day

which cannot be ignored. Hence live life with the hurdles and the smooth ground and term them

as challenges which will finally help you to discover 'YOURSELF' that which you hardly really

know.

Life is like a book, if opened you will find it interesting and valuable, if kept closed it collects

dust. Do not let the unfair barometer disappoint you and cast a shadow on the new beginning.

Open wide your eyes and fly against the storm, there is always a new dawn waiting.

Every effort has a fulfilment and in every weakness a rebuilding of strength.

Time is signalling you to fill the space and renew your thoughts, for every action is the governing

factor of your own thoughts. Life is the momentum of the present days. It never seems to be the

way one wants; it is for us to fill it with perfect moments. Let the days not hamper it. Try to

stretch your hands to broaden the horizon. Do not let the tormenting memories of failure block

the doors of hope. Failure does not mean that everything is lost; it means you must try a little

harder to prove yourself and find the hidden message of moving ahead.

"You are better than you are, if you know and read yourself".

Now here comes the time to repair, prepare for and answer the questions which were eluded.

What do I want?

Is it a correct choice?

Am I ready for it?

Let the questions ponder in your mind, if they are the new challenges that are facilitating and

empowering you to search or to just stop walking in the sun, yet remaining in the shade. Now is

the time to rediscover your healed self by putting your foot forward to go beyond the ordinary,

with an ocean of confidence in a newfound revolution in self.

Let us accept the fact that life is a moving machine remembering to measure each step,

minimising the hurdles that come your way and not forgetting to keep a positive attitude that

leads to victory. Make sure you decide and act with care and never forget that life is a filigree of

fine threads woven together intricately which needs to be handled carefully,......for such is life...

You Learn it – You know it.
You read it – You write it.
You make it – You find it.
You get it – You win it.

II
My Time... A Brief Connection

Before even completing my graduation, I was teaching English at St Ursula Girls High School

and Junior College Nagpur. I never wanted to take up the profession of teaching. I wanted to

become a doctor- a paediatrician, but luck brought me to school which today is a cherished

treasure from where I developed my personality. I learnt a number of things which have been

embedded in me.

When I recall my early days, I felt depressed, it burnt my desire to live. The silent sorrow and

Unshed tears came crumbling down crushing my dreams. I lost my way, the way which I had chosen from my childhood days, nothing seemed to be going in the right way, the way I wanted

it. It was a picture of faded paints.

As the moments, the hours, the days in school moved there was an incredible change, I was

enthralled by the motto of the school which said 'ARISE SHINE'. It had a magnetic effect on me,

and it changed my whole life.I found that everything I did was a promise of joy. My thoughts

vibrated, making me enjoy my work which sank deep into my system. Even before I realised

they settled as the pillars of strength. Those two little words helped overcome the previously

cherished dreams and led me to accept this marvellous opportunity. Though it was not what I

wanted but had drastically changed the scenario of my life.

My ambition became my past and what fell into my life blossomed. Little things grow, little lights

burn, little thoughts change, and a new avenue is born. If I had shied away from my present job

and continued to feel sorry for what I had lost, how would then I happily continue to serve this

prestigious institution, how would I have to be excellent in my field, how would I have been a recipient of the BestTeacher's State Award, and how would my students connect with me after decades and decades.

THIS WAS WHAT I WAS CALLED FOR. Life is to live in brightness and to polish it to shun darkness.

We must learn to accept what comes our way and lacquer to shine, rather than making life

miserable for what couldn't be achieved. Rabindranath Tagore rightly said, "If you cry because

the sun has gone out of your life, your tears will prevent you from seeing the stars".

Let us not forget...

Life is a momentum of the present days; life doesn't seem to be as we want it. We can fill it with

perfect moments, restyling our fears and stepping into our new arena made for us which we

couldn't and wouldn't want to see. Failure of the dream lost does not make one inferior and that

there is no chance to move. It surely means our limits have been increased to try hard to build a

life in line where the impossible has no space what-so-ever. But faith is ultimately to keep going,

it is what your life permits for it is an interweaving of fine threads assembled to be used with

great judgement.

My time – My space – My desire at times leads to the path of new situations and new success

but none could have realised it if the past situation had not risen. Hence the best way is to refine

life's journey and be prepared to face the challenges fearlessly.

I cited my brief journey of dreams which blossomed into a beautiful flower, as life presented

another path in the form of a new destination which brought new and pretty flowers of success

and joy gradually turned into life. Do not be discouraged if your dreams are not realised. Open

your eyes wide and you will find many paths to explore.

It's time we realise, we are programmed to learn things on our own. If we are unsettled in our

space, there is a crisis and our thinking seizes. Our limitations and strengths lie within us.

Someone rightly said, "If dreams are broken the cure is dream again and DEEPER."

III

Flying Against The Wind

"When you can learn from soft touches then you can learn from Hard Knocks."
If you cannot do great things in life do small things in a great way"

This is the next approach on how to tread your way through the scriptures of life and follow the

thematic approach which offers strength for our weaknesses, abandoning thoughts which are

repelling and leading to destruction.

Focus on the possibilities and not on fear. Frustration is understandable but it is better to know

that its effects on life are damaging and none will help you to throw open the windows to let in the ray of

hope. At times when life puts you in an uncontrollable situation, one needs to delve in and find

that fine line where other options are accessible.

It's here that you start searching for a glimpse of glowing light to find your way to recover. There

is a gush of wind and through the creek, light enters. Push with force and fly against the wind as

you repurpose yourself and ignore people's speculations.

Life is a beautiful journey in which circumstances differ. There are difficult, dangerous and

damaging obstacles which one is unable to face but there is also a tiny sparkling star within

each one of us, full of power to strike against the storm and which only needs to be ignited and

propelled with confidence and courage which will definitely result in the way to move forward.

Keep cool, cope with the anxious moments and walk into the path where credibility exists. It's

life, it is going to be hard but make every effort to take the best step. In case you miss one, don't

panic. Create a new path with a neutral approach. Remember, it needs to blossom to its full

potential only then will it be successful.

Now look beyond the boundary and enjoy the ride of life. In this world, everyone faces

problems. Those who are strong, stand with armour and face it, while those who are weaker in

comparison, tremble and succumb to it. To enlighten you again of the power, one has to use it

with a sound mind and strength, fasten your belts and free yourself from the chains of

unsuccessfulness, creating a new world for yourself.

Respect yourself, radiate yourself and gear yourself up to enter into an arena of joy and

accomplishment.

Don't ever say "Where do I go from here?"

Nothing happens quite by choice. You can climb the mountain and see nothing, but as you climb down, you will see the lush green pastures. So, now is the time to say "I can, therefore I am".

Design your own day or else someone else will.

Block out other's thoughts and dwell within your own mind and in your thinking. Refuse to be

discouraged. Believe in yourself and all that you are. Know that there is something inside, that is

greater than any obstacle.

Like never before, fly against the wind and hold on to the incandescent lamp called LIFE.

IV

To Unlock The Locked

Progress in life comes through taking initiative and continuing to find new strategies, plans and

concepts. THe original moment isn't enough to keep you moving. Your progress will grind to a

halt unless you try to unlock the lock.

Sweep the barren land, fill the engine with fuel of love, joy, peace, by controlling the

weaknesses and forming a strong pillar to rebuild and respond to the challenges faced.

The apparently hopeless situation is when we feel the closing of our wishes locked to perishable

thoughts that are being replaced by unknown ideas that are needed to mark the new beginning.

A right approach has to be taken or else the skeleton of negative thoughts will lead to

destructive conditions of self pity, failure, depression and dejection.

All of us are blessed with the power to tolerate in absolutely different ways and conditions. We

have to realise that every situation has a hidden benefit, hence our task is to discover and

rediscover, invent and reinvent the new arenas of thoughts, with faith and patience, leaving

behind the lurking dark obstacles and readily ushering in to the new start with hope.

It is not how much we can do, it is how we do it. We should know that silence is not golden all

the time, a few words pitched strongly with courage and determination will bring good results.

The big moment will come when you decide to find the right plot and learn how to think, how to

focus and move boldly. For this endless effort will make life more worth living. Further the

determination of not going down, the disappointment, the emptiness, the achievements to be

fulfilled, will need endless effort in order to receive the desired outcome.

Failure is one side of the coin. If faced with it, turn the key and open the windows to allow fresh

air to flow in. Don't be afraid to start again. This is the very chance again to build a concrete

path and let go of the temporary attachment.

The purpose of our life is not to make a living but to make a life. To feel the touch of the soft

wind to ease the mind, to feel the glimpse of life and to settle your thoughts to feel how living life

is, which is not only majestic and magnetic but also magical. Problems come and go, but

courage helps to solve them.

Results may take time but the desired effect may come, complete or partial. Be thankful that

they give us the opportunity to forge ahead.

Do not be afraid of problems, do not be afraid of failures nor be afraid of people's speculations.

Do not allow fear of any issue at any stage. Your task is to leap over the hurdles confidently and

start transforming yourself to live the right way, the way of enthusiasm and self care.

Life is the boatman that can take you to the shore safely. So build a connection with it, not

forgetting that after every storm, the sun comes with its light. Likewise for every problem, there

is a solution. So find it, solve it and celebrate it.

Usher in fresh air to find the purpose in life. Listen to the silence and it will bring the BEST

before your eyes.

V

Accept And Reject, Face It To Feel It

"If you make mistakes, have the courage to accept them"
Life is a challenge, Meet it!"

Never say tomorrow, the moment is always Now. Every second you are reborn with a new

beginning, so why wait, lead your ways with the ups and downs of life. The best way is to

confidently face the challenges put on the way by life. Learn to face it and learn to feel it. Time

waits for no one and continues in its own way. There can be revision of values in life but not of

time.

Be ready to face the unpredictable, don't turn back with the thought that nothing can be done

and end up being a loser which leads to the negativity of life and ultimately crashes to death.

Do we ever think that we have foolishly put our life by striking the match to burn secretly into ashes?, giving no time to think or feel the numbness we have created.

We panic with fruitless thoughts, being surrounded with our strong perceptions, weak and

contemplated mood and with a desire to put life into the box of nothing.

It is essential to keep a clean mind with good productive thoughts, strength to recover, simple

but wise attitude to follow - not forgetting that life is a part and parcel of smooth and rough roads

which have to be travelled cautiously.

Now to face life and to perceive it is unquestionably laborious and demanding but certainly not

impossible. Each one of us faces it, we all must do so fearlessly as life is a precious gift to be

treasured, loved and enjoyed, as we live life just once.

It's time to quash this stigma and refuse to let limitations stand in the way of our possibilities.

Move forward and confront the adversities, for this will give you the opportunity to improve and

grow. Past experiences bring doubt in the mind, so pack them away as they come to the

surface. Positivity advances in your direction, catch sight of it, reason out and don't lose sight of

it or else dark clouds will blind the mind if given space to self doubt, apathy and bitterness.

We must reminisce that most worries are enveloping things that may never occur but

unconsciously dwell in the mind and get entwined, reaching out to something inconceivable

bringing no relief but eventually leads to the termination of life.

This has a deep effect on those who are near and dear to us and they actually become the

loser. This advice is advisable to the weak and feeble and at times to the strong too.

Life is a challenge, go ahead-face it - feel it and have the intense quest to live, move from
ambiguity to certainty, not from certainty to ambiguity.

The great poet Rabindranath Tagore rightly said, "The sun rises every day but the sun set is
different."

A Summary Of Life –
One Real Reason: Life Is Not A Bed Of Roses
One Little Thought: Life Is Precious
One Realisation: Life Is Beautiful
A Test: Life Is A Jigsaw Puzzle
A Cup Of Emotions: Life Is Full Of Joy & Sorrows
A State Inevitable: Life Is To Live On...
Three Unchangeable Words: Life.Goes.On
It's time to reach out, for life has no pause buttons.

VI
The Balance/Time

*"Live with intentions. Trust your choices. Share your joy
and sorrow. Speak the truth"*
Tough times never last but tough people do"

Persevering and believing makes life sound and strong.
Everything depends on how you

balance the equation each day, each week, each month. There
will be thick and heavy clouds

hovering, bright rays of sun burning in the inner chamber of the
outer glittering world and a

jumble numble of countless big, wide and intriguing thoughts.

Can it be balanced with weak and inadequate strength or with a
confused and depressed mind?

No! It needs determination to face the painful crisis of life. The
balancing act has to be

programmed well. To equip yourself, these are the following
directives -

1. Prepare yourself to do it independently or with someone you
totally concur.

2. Revamp your space and your choice

3. Sow the seed of hope and determination

4. Despite the obstacles, move forward fearlessly

5. Seal the agony of the past

As you balance yourself with positivity, you begin with a triumphant start. You feel light, pleasant

as you acquaint yourself with new routes and ideas. You build a strong foundation for your life

as you make firm decisions with a balanced and cool mind.

Don't waste a single moment in transforming yourself and focus on right and appropriate

thinking thereby illuminating the signs of the new dawn. This strategy will make you capable of

dealing with both the external and internal confrontation of life.

This rebirth of balance will help in the bliss of realisation where one can believe and achieve

anything. Stand up for yourself, your mind has the ability to create and recreate. All it takes is to

start taking pride in all the struggles and looking forward to giving your best, stepping decisively

away from the excuses, while walking into the sense of satisfaction zone, taking a pledge to

tackle every situation with new aspirations.

Progress in life comes through taking initiative and continuing to press on with new designs,

new concepts, good plans enough to move forward. Our thoughts and words make us what we

are. In this there is growth within us. Remind yourself that you will grind to a halt unless you

refuel your engine.

It's time, to time the second before the second ticks away. Time to calm the mind by curtailing

the fluctuations, as one navigates the way through the thickness of the mind. Life cannot be

rewinded, it can only be reset to keep the balance well and under wraps.

Create a new and pleasant atmosphere and start giving your life an added measure of the

richness and contentment. Balance life and don't put your life on stake. Settle down, bury

doubts and fear. William Feather aptly said, "One way to get the most of life is to look upon it as an adventure."

VII
Build And Rebuild

Why do you think that life is a box of miseries?

Is it because we have missed the right opportunity or have not succeeded in what we wanted or

Is it the reason that your friends have achieved what you couldn't?

Refuse to let your imitations stand in the way of your possibilities. Let your determination

advance to build and rebuild a new pathway of undivided attention. The setback will in no way

be likeable but if you turn the table, it can bring a renewed commitment pushing back doubts

and unreasonable reasons to cite which indeed will hamper your opportunities of fulfilment and

the ability to trust yourself.

The joy you receive by rebuilding is not monetary, it is neither an alteration of thoughts. It is a new design, an endeavour to gain back the lost strength and to evacuate the uncertainty or the

non fulfilment of desire. Every human being has a unique strength to overcome problems, so

use value and come out of the unwilling thoughts that hamper your mind.

Let nothing daunt you. Recondition the weak moments with strong decisions and put your power

and stability to focus on yourself. Try not to take endless efforts to achieve excellence but to

break the shackles of uncertainty and scepticism and settle the unsettled with an honest effort to

live moment by moment and to shut the deadly panic which lurks in the mind.

Live NOW! Why search for happiness ; Happiness has no path, it is a path itself. This is a conscious period to leave behind the past and shape your own world. Retreat the incredible hidden gem raring to come out and fight against the gloomy span of time and thereby presenting the joy of living.

Search everyday, improve on the dark spots making efforts to see the richness of life When you

build and rebuild it transforms life and bridges the gap between joy of life and the staggering of

life.

It is rightly said, "the future belongs to those who believe that unless you have the courage, you

can't reach the shore."

You are the builder of your thoughts. Step ahead, there is no 'CAN'T', there is only 'CAN'.

VIII

Love The Life You Live

"The Known Today And And The Unknown Tomorrow,
Facts Are Many But The Truth Is One"

This is a profoundly sensitive line. Its output considerably stretches the big wide world - the

creation of God that must be pondered upon, reflected and realised silently and prayerfully -

What is life?

To know today is easy as we can see it, read it, learn it, mold it and rectify it. Tomorrow is an

unseen picture which may be imagined or written but its fullness is seen only if you open your

eyes when the sun rises the next day.

Life teaches you a lesson every moment, sometimes equipped with bright touches and

sometimes flows through unexpected sources. Looking at the world around the best step is to

create a paradigm to rejuvenate and to keep the fire burning with a need to be assertive in order

to get the desirable result.

Fill your life with twinkling stars. Today is your day, the spell of tomorrow is unknown. Never

hesitate to entrust the unknown future to the known God.

All your past experiences and your ruinous thoughts which lead to the termination of life must be

forcefully put to a screeching halt.

Not all are born great - grow the way it is meant to be. Make a wise choice. Happiness is

available, help yourself to it, don't regret the past, create your own opportunity, bring your own

ideas to life. Refuse to stop, you will gain. Discard fear and you will feel the pleasantries of life.

Insecurity, depression, anxiety will no way surround you.

Appreciate yourself. Failure is not something one doesn't have in life. You can't run away from it,

but you can powerfully crush it. Think before you act. Step into the clean, sparkling,

unpredictable life. Maybe tomorrow can also be yours.

Live at your own pace, life is not a race.

Precisely TODAY is definitely YOURS,
TOMORROW is QUESTIONABLE,
TODAY is NOW,
TOMORROW is DESTINY.

IX

The Great Moment

With the advancement of technology, man today is to be instructionally guided. Railway stations,

Bus terminus or airports have display devices that indicate the time of arrival and departure. But

the circle of life predicts only an arrival but never the departure of time.

We must understand and keep in mind that life is our golden period of time to be spent wisely

and with great gratitude to God.

Life is beautiful and a joy forever. Being happy doesn't mean everything around us is on a

smooth run. See beyond the imperfections to find peace. Living in the shadow of this colourful

world is not the purpose of living. Be prepared for all situations and create something that will be

of ultimate bliss.

Now how can you tell a story that is still being written?

It's time to wake up, fostering fortitude in times of struggle with a new view of thinking deeply

how one can flash the beacon of positivity.

Delight in being yourself. There is a difference between receiving and experiencing the value of

life. We all live in a world where love is the most precious virtue that exists. So the first thing is

to love yourself and appreciate your many blessings. Most of us have misunderstood the

meaning of life. Many of us think life is just living and feel life is just a circle which ends in death.

Here's what life analyses -

Life is not always happiness

Life is not external

Life not just a relationship

Life is not just sorrow

Life is not always bright sunlight

Life is not a lap of luxury

But

Life is an experience

Life is an expression

Life is learning

Life is loving

Life just goes on...

Life is a single word with much significance, diverse perspectives, never the same for everyone.

What is essential is to overcome hardships and failures. No doubt life is sometimes painful and

dry but each one of us is endowed with the power to endure.

Become your own best friend and see how life is easier. Every situation in life is temporary be it

good or not so good. Remember the not-so-good will not last forever, better days are on the

way. Think of what life has given rather than attempting to burn it because of unfulfilled desires and dreams.

Life is not measured by the breath we take but by moments that take your breath away. Don't

you think that life is too short to be anything but happy?

Life is a huge mirror, so strike a good pose, smile, for the place to be happy is HERE

JUST MAKE
Happiness a part of life
This is the fuel for thought
Reaching heights, steering right
Lets add sparkle to our life

X

The Beacon Of Hope

Nothing can dim the light that shines within you or from within you until you cross over the

bridge of insecurities. Life is woven by what you have and not by what is missing. You can't go

back and change the scenario but you can definitely start anew with what you have.

In doing so, you will find that the variation in the future life adds to a unique feeling of joy. This

we unknowingly recycled our unfinished aspirations.

We need to respect life, cherish it and create a canopy strong enough to hold the storm. Here

you find that HOPE and TRUST are two qualities that shield us from being enveloped by

detrimental thoughts which make one vulnerable to inaccuracy and at times blunder.

Having abandoned the conscious effort of being separate from the others or being a part of a whole, it's more like the importance of light in darkness or the deprival happiness of self and the

irony of being the shade of grey. Isn't it time to decide what we want to do with what we have?

Push your boundaries if you want to find a way to change your opinion of life. Evaluate yourself.

If there is an underlying hurt, wrong, confusion, or anger, cleanse it with clear perception and try

to think about the possibilities why it is lingering and then disconnect to connect with the right.

Decisions are always a hard choice when it comes to choosing between what you want and

what is right. We do not win every time, but there are always ways to recover. Start teaching

your mind to be strong to adversaries of life and patiently accept it. You will realise that you are

capable of facing it cautiously and boldly. Faith must join hands with work to acquire good

results.

There is often a lot more to recover than to cry over failures and jump into a conclusion that life

has nothing to give. If we look behind with understanding and before with hope and around us

with faith, we will make the crooked path smooth and trouble free.

So live life with a spectrum of brilliant colours, rejoice for life is just for once. Let the beacon of

hope,enrich your path. See things as they are, not as you want them to be. Let no time and life

slip from your fingers without paying the instrumental role we need to.

Life is a blend of smiles and cries
Savour it with acceptance
The sole thing to do now is–
Be alive when you are alive.

XI

The Last Page

The Last Page is always an invaluable treasure, for it deals with all the issues transparently with
sculpted reality.

Any situation in our life can have a negative outcome. We in common very easily fall prey to 'it'.

Thinking and trying to think deeply our mind gets hold of fear and frustration before anything has
happened.

One of the greatest truths you will ever learn is, if something untoward happens, it is because of
one's own negative thoughts and attitudes. Hence, we have to be strong to realise that every
situation has some benefits which we tend to overlook and forget.

We need to be free of confusion in mind that every confusion has to pass. We have to ponder
over some essential principles to get victory over the problems

i. Huge breakdowns

ii. Obstacles

iii. We cannot view anything good because dark clouds envelope us

iv. Life values tend to fall

v. Minds get berserk with questions

What is stored for me? Can I change my thinking?

Can I change my surroundings?

Why is my happiness deprived?

Will I ever get peace? Will I always be a loser?

Where and how can I get the answers?

The answers are with 'YOU' and You alone.

Surprised and bewildered! Yes, none can help you, none can be your guide, none can pacify

you, none can reassure you and finally a little bit of speculation will relate to you that you are in

a nutshell of fear and anguish.

Now it's time to listen to your inner voice and it will give you the Renaissance of life. Firstly what

I am and what I ever was, a harsh reality which flashes before your eyes and how you lost your

lifeline.

In seconds your mind speaks... I wish there was a way...

WELL

YES THERE IS...

In all that you do let 'LOVE' be the sole motive. Learn to create a new venue and look forward to

a world made better by 'YOU'. Keep in mind that behind the dark curtains there is a ray of right

called 'JOY'. But joy does not last nor does it end, it appears again and again to give you a

gentle reminder to go ahead with the beautiful journey of life letting go and moving on from what

no longer serves a positive purpose.

Do not forget the 3 Cs in life

CHOICE - CHANCE - CHANGE

You must make a CHOICE to take a CHANCE in your life or it will never CHANGE

A beautiful aspect of each one of our lives is living a life of enthusiasm and joy. Also to keep it

spreading the flavour of love and understanding to your parents, friends and those you meet. It is for 'YOU' to set the sail of life and explore the sea of opportunity, fly over with wings over the

ocean giving thanks to the creator who made you.

Finally,

The Last Page signifies –

LAST- Life Is An Adventure Special And Tender

PAGE - Perpetual Amazing Gracious Elegant